Does somebody need a hedgehug?

GIBBS SMITH

TO ENRICH AND INSPIRE HUMANKIND

Find what you love, and *gopher* it.

Sometimes you just have to say, "Who gives a *cluck!*"

Gulls just wanna have fun!

Whale always
be friends.

Looking *spot on,* girlfriend!

You are
*fin*tastic!

Let's get the *flock* outta here!

You're the best *dam* friend ever!

Owl always be there for you.

Never give up! Who *nose* what tomorrow will bring?

You *quack* me up!

Shake it off,
get going, and
keep *mooving*
forward.

Toucan

do it!

Iguana thank you for being part of my journey.

You make the
unbearable
bearable.

Our friendship just makes *scents.*

Girl, you're so *baaaaad* (but in a good way)!

Do no harm, but take no *bull.*

You *toadily* rock!

We *otter* get into trouble more often!

You've *goat* a friend in me.

I *ham* so glad
we're friends.

Live your life
with no *egrets*.

I can always
count on you to
let *minnow* the
truth.

Keep your *chins* up!

You were made

purrfect.

Does somebody
need a
hedgehug?

You can count on me when the *chimps* are down.

Keep calm
and get
philo*sloth*ical.

Ewe are my favorite human.

Sometimes you need to be a little *shellfish*.

You *moosen*'t forget how incredible you really are.

That *mastiff* been difficult, so treat yourself to some me time.

No *bunny* knows
me like you do.

Pray attention to your inner goddess.

Be confid*ant*,
jubil*ant*, and
triumph*ant*!

Don't just stand there, get out and *flamingle!*

Do the things
that *turtily*
make you happy.

Don't get *eaten* up by the little things.

First Edition
21 20 19 18 17   5 4 3 2 1

Text © 2017 Gibbs Smith

All rights reserved. No part of this
book may be reproduced by any means
whatsoever without written permission
from the publisher, except brief portions
quoted for purpose of review.

Published by
Gibbs Smith
P.O. Box 667
Layton, Utah 84041

1.800.835.4993 orders
www.gibbs-smith.com

Written by Anita Wood
Designed by Sky Hatter
Printed and bound in Hong Kong

Gibbs Smith books are printed on
either recycled, 100% post-consumer
waste, FSC-certified papers or on paper
produced from sustainable PEFC-
certified forest/controlled wood source.
Learn more at www.pefc.org.

Library of Congress Control Number:
2017935135
ISBN 978-1-4236-4810-9

Photo Credits

Photos from Shutterstock, © 2017 as follows:

Besjunior, 48
Tony Campbell, 52
Steve Cordory, 4
Rodrigo Cuel, 27
Davdeka, 76
Janossy Gergely, 59
Jianhao Guan, 75
Eric Isselee, front cover, back
cover, 11, 23, 51, 55, 79
Kjersti Joergensen, 20
Heiko Kiera, 32
Martin Kubista, 64

Anna Kucherova, 67
Brian Lasenby, 16
Paul Looyen, 35
Martin Mecnarowski, 40
MestoSveta, 68
Dudarev Mikhail, 43
nico99, 71
Labusova Olga, 3
Vadim Orlov, 36
Pakhnyushchy, 28
Chokchai Poomichaiya, 12
Lorna Roberts, 56

smereka, 24
spetenfia, 19
Stellina108, 63
Igor Stramyk, 44
sysasya photography, 47
Rachele Totaro IT, 60
tsuneomp, 8
Benjamin van der Spek, 15
Adam Van Spronsen, 31
Chris Watson, 7
Yusnizam Yusof, 72
Bildagentur Zoonar GmbH, 39